MEN IN

Chris Goode

MEN IN THE CITIES

OBERON BOOKS
LONDON

WWW.OBERONBOOKS.COM

First published in 2014 by Oberon Books Ltd
521 Caledonian Road, London N7 9RH
Tel: +44 (0) 20 7607 3637 / Fax: +44 (0) 20 7607 3629
e-mail: info@oberonbooks.com
www.oberonbooks.com

A catalogue record for this book is available from the British Library.

PB ISBN: 978-1-78319-167-3
E ISBN: 978-1-78319-666-1

Cover design by Dragonfly

Printed, bound and converted
by CPI Group (UK) Ltd, Croydon, CR0 4YY.

Men in the Cities was first performed at Traverse Theatre, Edinburgh on 31 July 2014

Writer / Performer – **Chris Goode**

Director – **Wendy Hubbard**

Designer – **Naomi Dawson**

Lighting Designer – **Katharine Williams**

Production Manager – **Hattie Prust**

Producer – **Ric Watts**

A Chris Goode & Company production
in association with Royal Court Theatre

Supported by Arts Council England

Thanks to:
Vicky Featherstone, Chris Campbell, Lucy Davies and all at the Royal Court; Orla O'Loughlin, Linda Crooks, Ruth McEwan, Claire Doohan and all at the Traverse; Richard Lee and all at Jerwood Space; Alex Markham; and Richard Davenport.

Special thanks to:
Eeva-Maria Mutka and Andy Paget for their kind hospitality during the final stages of writing this show.

ChrisGoodeandCompany

Chris Goode & Company is a collaboration between lead artist Chris Goode, producer Ric Watts, writer and critic Maddy Costa and a fluid ensemble of makers, designers and performers. At the heart of the ensemble is a core group of associate artists with whom we work more frequently.

Chris Goode & Company make theatre by creating welcoming spaces and interesting structures for unexpected things to happen in. We tell stories in ways that are both experimental and at the same time accessible and inclusive. And we think out loud about who we all are, hoping to catch a glimpse of how we might live better together.

Our principal aim is to make space for unheard voices. This is sometimes done by talking to people about their lives, and using their words to make their work. We often involve people in the imagining and making of our work who maybe don't think of themselves as artists. We are increasingly recovering and presenting lost or neglected work by artists (both historical and contemporary) whose lives and thoughts have led them to be marginalised or overlooked. And we create bold original work that represents queer, dissident and politically nonconformist perspectives.

Since forming in 2011, Chris Goode & Company has created a body of work that includes: *STAND* (Oxford Playhouse), *Monkey Bars* (Unicorn Theatre / Traverse Theatre), *9* (West Yorkshire Playhouse), *The Forest & The Field* (Ovalhouse), *GOD/HEAD* (Ovalhouse and Theatre in the Mill), *The Adventures of Wound Man & Shirley* (Edinburgh, BAC and touring), *Keep Breathing* (Drum Theatre Plymouth) and *Open House* (West Yorkshire Playhouse / Mayfest). The company is currently making a number of new shows, including *Albemarle* (developing at West Yorkshire Playhouse) and *Longwave* (house Recommission).

To find out more about Chris Goode & Company, and our work, past present and future, please visit www.chrisgoodeandcompany.co.uk or follow us on Twitter @chrisgoodeandco

Lead Artist: Chris Goode

Producer: Ric Watts

Critic-in-Residence: Maddy Costa

Associate Artists: Angela Clerkin, Jo Clifford, Wendy Hubbard, James Lewis, Pauline Mayers, Jamie Wood.

Advisory Board: Lilli Geissendorfer, Wendy Hubbard, Judith Knight, Emma Stenning, Martin Sutherland.

THE ENGLISH STAGE COMPANY
AT THE ROYAL COURT THEATRE

The Royal Court is the writers' theatre. It is a leading force in world theatre, finding writers and producing new plays that are original and contemporary. The Royal Court strives to be at the centre of civic, political, domestic and international life, giving writers a home to tackle big ideas and world events and tell great stories.

The Royal Court commissions and develops an extraordinary quantity of new work, reading over 3000 scripts a year and annually producing around 14 world or UK premieres in its two auditoria at Sloane Square in London. Over 200,000 people visit the Royal Court each year and many thousands more see our work elsewhere through transfers to the West End and New York, national and international tours, residencies across London and site-specific work, including recent Theatre Local Seasons in Peckham, King's Cross and Haggerston.

The Royal Court's extensive development activity encompasses a diverse range of writers and artists and includes an ongoing programme of writers' attachments, readings, workshops and playwriting groups. Twenty years of pioneering work around the world means the Royal Court has relationships with writers on every continent.

The Royal Court opens its doors to radical thinking and provocative discussion, and to the unheard voices and free thinkers that, through their writing, change our way of seeing. "With its groundbreaking premieres and crusading artistic directors, the Royal Court has long enjoyed a reputation as one of our most daring, seat-of-its-pants theatres." The Times "The most important theatre in Europe." *New York Times*

Within the past sixty years, John Osborne, Arnold Wesker and Howard Brenton have all started their careers at the Court. Many others, including Caryl Churchill, Mark Ravenhill and Sarah Kane have followed. More recently, the theatre has found and fostered new writers such as Polly Stenham, Mike Bartlett, Bola Agbaje, Nick Payne and Rachel De-lahay and produced many iconic plays from Laura Wade's *Posh* to Bruce Norris' *Clybourne Park* and Jez Butterworth's *Jerusalem*. Royal Court plays from every decade are now performed on stage and taught in classrooms across the globe.

NAOMI DAWSON trained at Wimbledon School of Art and Kunstacademie, Maastricht. Designs with Chris Goode: *STAND* (Oxford Playhouse); *The Forest and the Field* (Oval House and tour); *Monkey Bars* (Unicorn, Traverse); *9* (West Yorkshire Playhouse); *Keep Breathing, King Pelican, Speed Death of the Radiant Child* (Drum Theatre, Plymouth); *…Sisters* (Gate/Headlong); *Landscape and Monologue* (Ustinov, Bath). Other theatre include: *Beryl, Mary Shelley* (West Yorkshire Playhouse); *Hotel, Three More Sleepless Nights* (NT); *The Roaring Girl, As You Like It, King John* (RSC); *Dancing at Lughnasa, In Praise of Love* (Theatre Royal, Northampton); *Fanny och Alexander, Love and Money* (Malmo Stadsteater); *Y Storm* (Theatr Genedlaethol Cymru); *Speechless, The Glass Menagerie* (Shared Experience); *Blue Sky* (Pentabus/Hampstead); *Belongings* (Hampstead/Trafalgar Studios); *Amerika, Krieg der Bilder*(Staatstheater Mainz); *Scorched* (Dialogue/Old Vic Tunnels); *The Typist* (Sky Arts); *The Gods Weep* (RSC/ Hampstead); *Rutherford and Son* (Northern Stage); *The Container* (Young Vic); *Amgen: Broken* (Sherman Cymru); *If That's All There Is* (Lyric); *State of Emergency, Mariana Pineda* (Gate); *Stallerhof, Richard III, The Cherry Orchard, Summer Begins* (Southwark Playhouse); *Phaedra's Love* (Young Vic/Barbican Pit); *Different Perspectives* (Contact Theatre); *Market Tales* (Unicorn); *Attempts on Her Life, Widows, Touched* (BAC); *Home, In Blood, Venezuela, Mud, Trash, Headstone* (Arcola); *A Thought in Three Parts* (Burton Taylor). Forthcoming designs include: *The White Devil* (RSC).

CHRIS GOODE is a writer and theatre maker, and the lead artist of Chris Goode and Company.

With CG&Co, his work has included: the Fringe First award-winning *Monkey Bars* (Unicorn Theatre, Traverse Theatre and UK tour); *STAND* (Oxford Playhouse); *The Albemarle Sketchbook* (Transform '14 at West Yorkshire Playhouse); *The Forest and the Field* (Ovalhouse and UK tour); *The Adventures of Wound Man and Shirley* (BAC); *9* (WYP); *GOD/HEAD* (Ovalhouse and UK tour); *Open House* (WYP / Mayfest / NT Studio); *Where We Meet* (home performance, Edinburgh Fringe); *Hippo World Guest Book* (UK tour); and *Keep Breathing* (Drum Theatre, Plymouth).

Outside the company, his work has included two other Fringe First award-winning shows: *Neutrino* (with Unlimited Theatre: Soho Theatre and international tour); and his own solo debut *Kiss of Life* (Drill Hall), which in 2007 travelled to Sydney Opera House as part of the Sydney International Festival. In 2008 he won the inaugural Headlong / Gate New Directions Award for his production *…SISTERS* at the

Gate Theatre. In 2010-11 he was part of the international touring cast of Tim Crouch's play *The Author*.

Other notable recent work as, variously, writer, director, deviser and performer, has included: *MAD MAN*, *King Pelican* and *Speed Death of the Radiant Child* (all Drum Theatre, Plymouth); *Infinite Lives* (Tobacco Factory, Bristol); *Weird Sisters* (Camden People's Theatre); the Total Theatre award-winning *The Worst of Scottee* (Roundhouse and international tour); *The Loss of All Things* (as part of *66 Books* at the Bush); *Who You Are* (Tate Modern) and *Where You Stand* (Contact Theatre, Manchester); *Glass House* (Royal Opera House Covent Garden); *Landscape / Monologue* (Ustinov, Bath); *Hey Mathew* (Theatre in the Mill, Bradford); *Longwave* (Lyric, Hammersmith). Between 2009-13 he also made a number of fugitive works in collaboration with Jonny Liron under the duo name Action one19.

In autumn 2014 Oberon will publish Chris's *The Forest and the Field*, a book about theatre. Other publications include *The History of Airports: Selected texts for performance 1995-2009*, and, as editor, *Better Than Language: An anthology of new modernist poetries*, both published by Ganzfeld. He continues to blog at Thompson's Bank of Communicable Desire, and hosts the podcast Thompson's Live.

WENDY HUBBARD is a director, dramaturg, and researcher. Wendy is an associate artist and advisory board member of Chris Goode & Company. Recent work with the company includes *The Adventures of Wound Man and Shirley* (National Tour, 2011-12), *God/Head* (2012), and *The Forest and the Field* (2013). Other recent directing includes Jamie Wood's *Beating McEnroe* (2013), Tom Lyall's *Defrag* (2012) and work as Outside Eye and Collaborator on Melanie Wilson's *Autobiographer* (2011) and *Landscape II* (2013). Theatre projects in development include *Ono!* with Jamie Wood and *Interregnum*, a new immersive show about iconoclasm and the English Civil War, co-directed with Gemma Brockis (Shunt). Previous work as co-director of theatre company Mapping4D includes *The Pink Bits* (winner of the OSBTT Award, Riverside Studios, 2004). Wendy is researching a PhD at Queen Mary, University of London.

HATTIE PRUST is a London-based production and stage manager working in theatre and performance art. She is coming straight into this project from production managing the national tour of Bryony Kimmings' award-winning show *Credible Likeable Superstar Role Model*. Other recent artists and companies Hattie has worked with include: Scottee Inc, Dickie Beau, Peggy Shaw, Duckie, Lucy Hutson, Amy Lamé, Penny Arcade, Fuel, Figs in Wigs, Pacitti Company and AiR Project. Hattie is also a founding member of the arts collective AiR Supply.

RIC WATTS is a producer based in Manchester. He is co-founder of Chris Goode & Company and has produced all of the company's work to date. Ric is also Producer for Unlimited Theatre (resident company at West Yorkshire Playhouse) for whom he has produced *Play Dough, MONEY the game show, The Noise, Mission To Mars* and *The Giant & The Bear;* for Analogue, for whom he has produced *Mile End, Beachy Head, Lecture Notes on a Death Scene, 2401 Objects, Re-enactments* and the upcoming projects *Transports, Stowaway* and *Sleepless*; and for the collaborations between Chris Thorpe and Hannah Jane Walker, including *The oh fuck moment* and *I Wish I Was Lonely*. Ric has previously produced and toured work by Ridiculusmus, Kazuko Hohki, theimaginarybody, The TEAM, Filter Theatre, Schtanhaus, The Frequency D'ici, Laura Mugridge, Royal & Derngate, The Other Way Works and the Queer Up North International Festival. He is currently on the board of directors of Cartoon de Salvo, on the Steering Group for RashDash and the Large Arts Awards panel for The Wellcome Trust.

KATHARINE WILLIAMS is a lighting designer working in drama, dance and physical theatre, with some opera, musical and circus projects. She works in the UK and internationally. Her designs have been seen in China, Hong Kong, New Zealand, Canada, the USA, Mexico, Ireland, Holland, Spain, Italy, Germany, Armenia, Romania, Russia and the Czech Republic. Credits include: *Death Actually* (Toynbee Hall); *North* (Summerhall); *Dealer's Choice* (Royal and Derngate); *Mad Man* (Plymouth Theatre Royal); *Billy The Girl* (Clean Break Theatre); *Moominland Winter* (Theatre Royal Bath); *Medea* (Actors of Dionysus); *The Noise* (Unlimited Theatre); *The Ruling Class* (English Theatre Frankfurt); *A Midsummer Night's Dream*, *Cyrano De Bergerac* and *Othello* (Grosvenor Park Open Air Theatre); *Address Unknown* (Soho Theatre); *Not I* (Royal Court); *Say It With Flowers* (Sherman Cymru); *Resonance At The Still Point Of Change*

(Southbank Centre); *Heidi – A Goat's Tail* (Theatre Royal Bath); *Ballroom Of Joy And Sorrows* (Watford Palace Theatre); *Krapp's Last Tape, Spoonface Steinberg* (Hull Truck); *Anne And Zef* (Company of Angels); *God/Head* (Chris Goode & Company); *The French Detective And The Blue Dog* (Bath Theatre Royal); *The Westbridge* (Royal Court); *Invisible* (Transport Theatre); *The Pajama Men* (Assembly Theatre); *CLOSER* (Théâtre des Capucins); *Faeries* (Royal Opera House); *Landscape & Monologue* (Theatre Royal Bath); *Ivan And The Dogs* (ATC/Soho Theatre); *The Goat, Or Who Is Sylvia?* (Traverse Theatre), *Reykjavic* (Shams); *Nocturnal* (The Gate); *Amgen:broken* (Sherman Cymru/Theatr Clywd); *Dolls* (National Theatre of Scotland); *I Am Falling* (Gate Theatre/Sadler's Wells); *Touched For The Very First Time* (Trafalgar Studios).

This text went to press before the end of rehearsals and so may differ slightly from the play as performed.

The UK suicide rate was 11.6 deaths per 100,000 population in 2012, but there are significant differences in suicide rates between men and women. Male suicide rates were more than three times higher at 18.2 male deaths compared with 5.2 female deaths per 100,000 population.

– Office of National Statistics, press release, 18 February 2014

Whoever is without a home, will never have one now.

– Rainer Maria Rilke, 'Autumn Day'

I'm a stranger here

I'm a stranger everywhere

I would go home, but honey

I'm a stranger there

– 'I'm A Stranger Here' (traditional song)

1.

Hey. How's everyone doing?

This is a story called *Men in the Cities*.

It starts in the middle of the night, with the sound of screaming. This awful kind of shrieking sound.

It's a fox out in the street, it's a vixen. Being fucked. Do you know that sound? It's a city sound, these days. It sounds like murder, like the worst distress.

The sound of that screaming vixen in the road outside tears into the dream of Rod Palladino as he sleeps alone in a king-size bed. If you ask Rod Palladino he'll tell you he doesn't dream, and you'd probably say, man, everybody dreams, and he'd soften a bit and say, I don't remember. I can never remember what I dreamt about.

The scream of the vixen being fucked in the street outside enters Rod Palladino's dream like a scimitar tearing through a cinema screen and suddenly he's dreaming about his own son as a baby. His son Freddie, who in life is seven years old now and doesn't like being called The Fredster any more but in the dream is a baby. And Rod's trying to get him to sleep, in the dream, and he's laid him in a drawer in a chest of drawers, and he's crying and crying, and Rod's trying to get the drawer shut. But the baby's head is too big to go in. Rod's slamming the head in the

drawer, slamming, and the head is crumpling, like
papier mache, no blood just smashed, and the dark
black O of Freddie's mouth is screaming with the
voice of the vixen outside in the street. Fuck me, goes
the vixen. Fuck me, more.

If you Google 'vixen crying mating call' there's a
thing that says: don't be frightened when you hear the
vixen's scream, the scream is only a love song. It's only
to human ears that it sounds like murder.

On waking, Rod Palladino will genuinely not
remember this dream.

The first alarm to go off is Rehan's at five forty a.m. It
used to feel early when he started out but now it just
feels like a fact, like any other fact in the fact-based
universe.

He sits on the edge of the bed looking at his bare
feet. Some days he thinks about praying but he never
actually prays. He thinks about his toenails. They
don't look right. And anyway what's the difference
between thinking about praying and actually praying?

When he brushes his teeth there's blood in his spit,
just enough to make the spat-out toothpaste a little
bit pink. Pink mint spit. He should probably floss like
his dentist says. But then you look at Napoleon. Jerry
Lee Lewis. Muhammad Ali. You wouldn't catch them
flossing. Maybe Ali. He had good teeth in his day.

Dale's alarm goes off at five to six. Almost before he's heard the sound, he hits snooze.

Tom's radio comes on at one minute to six which gives him a minute to come to before the six o'clock news. Some mornings it's OK but this particular morning he feels like he's climbing out of a well, like he slept all night at the bottom of a well.

Albert's alarm goes off at six. For some reason it's much louder than usual. It frightens the life out of him. Talbot, the dog, comes to see if everything's all right. Albert's heart is racing. Talbot can probably hear that the blood in Albert is going round Albert a bit too fast.

Tom listens to the voice on the radio saying: it's six o'clock on the morning of Thursday 23rd May 2013, and here are the headlines, and Tom remembers the terrible news from the evening before, and he doesn't want to listen, but he listens, because you don't get to choose what the news is.

Paul's alarm goes off at ten past six in the middle of a song in his head. This song has been playing in his head all night. A song from infant school. He hasn't thought about it for forty years. 'When A Knight Won His Spurs'. There are words in the song that he hardly ever hears anymore and they glow, somehow, in the lyric, like they're radioactive. Words like 'gallant', and 'valour', and 'steed'.

Dale's alarm goes off again at six fifteen. He hits snooze again, but it's never as nice as the first snooze.

Tom listens to the business news and it reminds him, as usual, of when the cool kids used to huddle in the corner of the classroom at break and talk about girls as if girls as a category were a sort of bank heist they were planning.

Rehan burns the toast. He scrapes it into the sink for a bit and then he goes: What the fuck am I doing, what the fuck, I'm a forty-four year old man, and he throws the toast away in the pedalbin. He'll have a cereal bar when he gets downstairs.

Jeff's radio alarm is set for six thirty but he's been awake since five and just lying there so as soon as the radio comes on he turns it off. 'We're going to be talking,' says the radio presenter in the two half-seconds he's audible. No we're not, says Jeff, out loud, to no one.

Talbot does his morning business, sweet as a nut. Albert's a little bit fond of Talbot's shit. It's like, that's my boy.

Lying in bed, thinking, Jeff suddenly notices how quiet it is. There used to be a milkman but he stopped. Jeff whistles a happy tune. He doesn't notice that the happy tune he whistles is the one about whistling a happy tune, so no one will suspect you're afraid.

Downstairs, in the shop, Rehan takes his Stanley knife and starts cutting open the day's newspaper bundles. TERROR RETURNS TO BRITAIN, says one of the headlines. Oh terror, thinks Rehan. I didn't even notice you'd gone away.

Dale's alarm goes off again at six thirty-five. He hits snooze again. This day and age, he thinks, a man doesn't get to hit much, not with impunity. You hit snooze.

Tom starts the shower running. He takes off his vest, and his pyjama bottoms, and he stands naked in front of the bathroom mirror. I am a naked man, thinks Tom. Luckily, the mirror only comes down as far as his neck. He looks at his grey stubble in the mirror.

YOU PEOPLE WILL NEVER BE SAFE, says another headline. There's a bit of cereal bar stuck in Rehan's teeth. He can't get it out with his tongue. It's going to be that sort of day. BLOOD ON HIS HANDS, HATRED IN HIS EYES. That's another headline. Also, the scratchcards need replenishing. It never rains, thinks Rehan. He's never in his whole life heard anyone finish that proverb. He thinks that's it. 'It never rains.' It means it never rains so you're always parched. It never rains so everything turns to dust.

Jeff has an ulcer on his gum. He can't leave it alone. It feels enormous.

Lots of alarms at seven o'clock, all over town, Toby in his new flat and Che sleeping on his mate's floor and Anthony who didn't get to bed till four because Powerpoint 14.0 is a twat, and Graeme who has never got out of the habit of rising early, though he's been retired for seven years and no one would begrudge him a lie-in.

Graeme thinks for a moment on waking about the boy in *The Neverending Story*. He comes into his mind like an urgent phone call. The boy and the white horse sinking in the swamp. He's a good actor, that boy. Noah Hathaway. The giant talisman around his neck, between his little nipples. Was the horse called Artex? Surely not. Whatever happened to Noah Hathaway? Apart from the inevitable. Noah Hathaway, thinks Graeme. He certainly hath.

7.02. Rehan opens up. Derrick is waiting.

– You're two minutes late, bruv, says Derrick.

– Ah, you're dead a long time, says Rehan.

– I thought your lot believed in reincarnation, says Derrick.

– Not my lot, says Rehan. I mean I'll come back if there's the option, don't get me wrong.

– What as, says Derrick?

– I don't know, says Rehan. A prawn.

– I thought your lot weren't allowed shellfish, says Derrick.

– Not my lot, says Rehan.

– Why a prawn then? says Derrick. As a prawn in the ocean you swallow a lot of shit, you know.

– As a newsagent you swallow a lot of shit, my friend, says Rehan. But a prawn? No business rates.

Derrick picks up his usual paper. The headline says: quote: 'We killed this British soldier. It's an eye for an eye.' End quote.

– I'd pull the lever myself, says Derrick.

– This is it, says Rehan.

They both look at the man on the front page. His beanie hat. The blood on his hands. Cool trainers.

Ben cuddles up to Matthew. He should have got up with the alarm at seven but a few more minutes won't hurt. Not today.

– Baby move your elbow, says Matthew. It's digging into me.

– Sorry, says Ben, and he moves his arm and he kisses Matthew's shoulder through his Cookie Monster T-shirt.

– You're nice, says Matthew.

Just five more minutes. Like that. Like two boys in a den. As if no one in the world would know where to find them. As if they'd run away together and made this den. A place to tell stories in. A place to suck each other's cocks and tell stories and talk about the wideness of the world. The wilderness, the wildness inside.

Jeff looks at his Bran Buds. I did National Service for this, he thinks.

For a moment he wonders about frying himself an egg. A couple of eggs. Fried bread.

But didn't he used to say to Annie, what's the point in having a routine if you're not going to stick to it? And she used to say to him, you've only one heart, you'd better look after it, and it will look after you. After forty years that's how you talk to each other. Dozens and dozens of catchphrases.

He looks at the calendar on the kitchen wall. One of those long thin engagement calendars, with a picture at the top of each page of the Lost Gardens of Heligan. Christ, thinks Jeff, aren't months long.

– Why didn't you wake me?, Matthew's saying as he jumps around putting his suit trousers on.

– Baby you were awake, says Ben.

– You know what I mean, says Matthew.

– I hate watching you get dressed, says Ben. It's just wrong. I wish you were my slave. I'd make you be naked all the time.

Matthew tucks his shirt in.

Eight o'clock. Rufus is still in bed.

On the screen of his smartphone, two American youths in their early twenties are undressing each other in the locker room of a high school gymnasium.

Rufus squeezes his genitals with his free hand.

He just wants them to get to the fucking part. Enough kissing. Blah. He hasn't got all day.

One of the boys is blond and one of them has dyed black hair. They're both really thin. The one with the black hair also has black steel ear stretchers and a Thundercats tattoo on his shoulder and a five-pointed star just above his groin and both boys are totally shaved because the site's called Gay Twink Angels and everyone knows angels aren't hairy.

– Stop nuzzling, you pussies, says Rufus to his phone. He rubs his other hand on his cock. If I wanted to watch people falling in love, he says, I'd go to the fucking park.

He skips forward a bit and his phone does buffering for a while.

– Fuck that, says Rufus to his phone. Fucking buffering.

He's woken up with a headache.

The video resumes with a low-angle shot of a studded tongue circling a fat sleek cock.

– Cool, says Rufus, flicking his own erection with his thumb.

– Rufus mate! shouts Rufus's stepdad from downstairs.

Fuck sake, thinks Rufus.

– You up yet?

– Yeah totally, shouts Rufus.

– Better get a wiggle on, shouts his stepdad. You want to open your presents before school.

Fuck it, thinks Rufus. He throws back his duvet and looks at his dick sticking up like a sundial. He gobs at it. Direct hit. Awesome.

Fucking come on then, thinks Rufus. You never know, there might be some all right presents in there somewhere. And anyway, it's not every day you turn ten years old. Come on.

– Oh can you send me a text to remind me to get laundry stuff?, says Matthew as he leans in to kiss Ben.

– Sure, says Ben. That's it. That was it. That kiss.

– I won't be late.

– Love you, says Ben.

– Love you babe, says Matthew, round the corner.

Kiss me again, Ben doesn't say. It doesn't make any difference. It wouldn't. Another kiss wouldn't make any difference.

What a terrible thing to know.

Graeme sits down on the piano stool. The book he's been working his way through is already open in front of him. It's called *Thirty Tiny Pieces*. And then, underneath, in smaller letters: *For Little Learners*.

It was already a bit old-fashioned when he first got given it. Christmas 1957. It's hard to believe that there's anyone still alive who lived in that world.

Today's piece is called 'Brushing the Teeth'. It says it's to be played 'vigorously, but cheerfully'. You'll take it as you get it, thinks Graeme.

But he has a crack at it. It's not quite right. He hasn't noticed that's supposed to be an F sharp all the way through. But one has to look on this as a long-term project. One day, 'Brushing the Teeth' will be a distant memory, fondly recalled, if at all.

Dale throws up on the way to the bathroom.

Rufus says thanks for his new bike, though what the fuck he's supposed to do with a bike, like fucking ride it around like a tool or something.

Ben starts to run a bath. For some reason he just wants to have a bath. There's something about the way you just lie there. Sort of waiting and sort of not.

Jeff arrives at the house he's decorating. Herself's out for the day so she's left the key on the back of the bird feeder. He lets himself in, puts the kettle on, puts the radio on.

Rehan's listening to the same radio station in the shop.

The man in the clip sounds very calm and composed as he says:

The only reason we have killed this man today is because Muslims are dying daily by British soldiers. And this British soldier is one.

Jeff, on his own in the kitchen, has to sit down for a moment, and when the kettle boils, he doesn't get up.

Ben tests the bath water. It's a bit too hot. Whatever. He lowers himself down into it, and it stings. All over his body it stings.

Matthew arrives at work feeling thirsty from the bus. He goes straight to the water cooler. He's forgotten, but is quickly reminded, that they've got new cups for the water. They're not even cups. They're cones. With a point at the bottom. So you can't put them down. It's like they're minimizing the time you're holding the cup before you throw it away. Like, this cup fucking only really exists to be discarded.

Matthew's line manager comes over to the water cooler. Matthew's trying to develop an easier relationship with this guy. Little bit of banter maybe.

– What's up with these cones?, says Matthew. He's about to launch into ninety seconds of brilliant observational comedy.

– They're a load bloody cheaper, says Matthew's line manager. And then they're just standing there.

Ben is lying in the bath, letting his body become reconciled to the temperature of the water. It's actually kind of nice.

He looks at his long body lying there in front of his face, with his feet up on the edge of the bath either side of the taps. He looks at his toes. Bodies are weird.

He doesn't have a hard-on but he sort of does. He holds his cock in his hand and smiles to himself. He's thinking about the first time he and Matthew slept together. Three years ago. Nineteen and eighteen. Ben, circumcised, and Matthew, not, so they sort of compared, and Matthew said a bunch of weirdly angry stuff about circumcision and how it was a kind of butchery and wasn't Ben fucking furious to have had this inflicted on him before he could consent or…, and Ben had had to just trust that this wasn't anti-Semitism, this was just Matthew really liked foreskins. Or maybe that's just love, Ben thinks now. Having someone lying next to you at night murmuring in your ear about all the things that are supposed to hurt, that you hadn't even thought about before.

And then they did this ventriloquist routine with their cockholes which ended up with their dicks singing 'Letter From America' by the Proclaimers.

And no one, not even Ben, knew Ben's cock better than Matthew. So that's, what is that kind of knowledge. To know someone's body. Their hidden, their whatever, the taste of them, their secrecy, what does that mean?

Because it doesn't carry forward, does it, into the… Into the whatever else means anything.

There's just separateness. There's just the shortfall.

That's Ben's phone. Who will that be who wants to know why he hasn't turned up for work?

The ringtone ends. And Ben holds his breath and pinches his nose and shuts his eyes and sinks down under the water and just hangs out like he's a baby waiting to be born.

And when he comes back up in a hurry and breathes and breathes and breathes, someone is calling his phone again, and it's time. And that's fine.

Jeff listens to the ten o'clock news on the radio. He hasn't moved since the nine o'clock news. Hasn't started work. He hasn't even noticed the hour go by.

They're playing a different bit of the footage now. The killer's rant, they're calling it. They play a bit that goes:

Why do you call us extremists and kill us? You lot are extreme. You are the ones that when you drop a bomb you think it hits one person? Or rather your bomb wipes out a whole family?

Jeff takes a pink felt tip out of a pot on the kitchen table and on his hand he writes the word: 'ATTIC'.

And then he crosses it out because he doesn't want anyone to see that he's written it.

And then he licks his thumb and rubs out the ink because it's more bright pink than he thought it would be.

But it leaves a blotch and he'll remember what the blotch means when he gets home.

Graeme can't quite face going out and doing errands, so he sits in his armchair and has a go at yesterday's cryptic crossword.

Rufus scratches a little crucifix into his arm with a pair of compasses. It's not very big but it bleeds a bit. He's not even sure what lesson this is. It's about plants breathing or some wank. What is that, geography?

Brian takes off his glasses and rubs the bridge of his nose. He's new to this story. He's an architect. The sort that designs buildings that are designed not to be noticed. No one really touches Brian's face apart from Brian and his barber and his dentist maybe and his optician, and if they touch his face they probably apologize.

Ben has got a playlist up together on iTunes. He reckons three hours of music should be enough to see this through but he puts it on repeat just in case.

He's still naked from the bath and a little bit damp but it means he can feel his body moving through the air of the bedroom and it's definitely him.

He's done some research. An overdose of painkillers alone is unlikely to be effective. But he's got some old antidepressants to chuck in and he's going to tape a bag over his head: which reminds him: he's got to write something down somewhere that says this was not a sex game that went wrong. Except it doesn't matter does it. And anyway, fucking life is a sex game that went wrong.

He starts with the paracetamol. Pushes them all out of their blister packs. Thirty-six tablets. It's a start. And a big carton of Ribena because apparently you want something sweet.

He sets this first batch of tablets out in a square on the table. Six rows of six. And he looks at them. And then he rearranges them. Four rows of nine. And he looks at them again, and then he does three rows of twelve. Two rows of eighteen. And then he settles on one long line of thirty-six. One by one. Like a time axis.

In the movies you see people swallow fistfuls at once but that's not what he wants. He wants orderly. One at a time. Because then if a little voice pops up and says, Stop it, Ben, this isn't right, it's not too late to stop and think.

The bag and the parcel tape. The other pills. The Ribena and the glass. The rest of the bedroom. Clothes in the wardrobe. Books on the table. The window, and through it, some sort of outside world kind of thing.

One by one. Starting with one. Waiting for the little voice to pop up.

Two. Three.

And it doesn't pop up. It doesn't, it doesn't. It just keeps not popping up.

There's a point where he thinks, fuck I need to text Matthew to get laundry stuff. So he texts him. LAUNDRY STUFF exclamation mark exclamation mark, kiss kiss. But he doesn't press send. Feels a bit wrong to send that. Like that would be weird.

Graeme's out doing his errands.

Graeme's sitting room, without Graeme, just for a little while. The piano with its lid open. The books, and the videos, proper old video cassettes, several without labels, just marks on the spine, little hieroglyphs that only Graeme understands. The cut flowers in two corners, the cottagey lampshades, the fruitbowl with its patient fruit. The glass saucer with pebbles on it and the button box.

On the table next to Graeme's armchair, a saucer with an empty teacup on it and half of a ginger oatcake. And the cryptic crossword neatly completed in a steady hand. Very impressive. And then you pick it up and look at it, and according to Graeme, the answers go:

FELCHES / ORGAN GRINDER / SPANK / TITPLAY / FRENULUMS / BABY BEL / SPUNK INK / NUDE BURGLAR / ASS FART / SPANIEL / GIRLCOCK / POTIPHARS COCK / BANGS / FECULENCE / LIONEL BLUE / YMCA SKANK / PENI WART / SPAG HOOPS / GORGE / TICKLER / VAG MARMALADEEE / CUB RAPE / PUBE and ODOUR EATERS.

The song that's going through Graeme's head as he goes about his errands is 'Morning Has Broken'.

Such a shame, he thinks, what happened to Cat Stevens.

Thank fuck no one at school has noticed it's Rufus's birthday. He doesn't want the bumps. He doesn't

want cake. He wants Arthur. Arthur from the class
next door who is tall and dark and lean and his eyes
have this light in them. And he has this knack of
wearing his clothes in a way that makes you just
think all the time about his clothes and his body
underneath them, and he comes to school with
bruises sometimes so you see his body in PE and the
teacher says: Been in the wars again Arthur?, and it's
fucking hot.

At morning break it takes a certain amount of
telepathic staring but eventually Arthur goes into
the playground toilets and Rufus walks across the
playground in a half-suppressed hurry. But Arthur's
just gone in to splash some water on his face so by the
time Rufus gets there, Arthur's coming out again, and
Rufus is like fuck my life.

But Faisal's having a piss, little Faisal who sings in
the front row of the choir so you get to see inside
his mouth a lot, and Rufus goes and stands next to
Faisal and blatantly looks down at him doing what
he's doing and he says something to Faisal that Faisal
doesn't even understand and then his hand's on the
back of Faisal's head, rubbing the back of his head,
and then there's just this roar in Rufus's mind, like
in those warning films the fire brigade do where they
drag a sofa out into a car park and set fire to it just to
show you what can go wrong and how quickly and
how totally and for ever and no one will ever love you
again.

Graeme's half-eaten oatcake just sitting on its saucer.
Let's look at that for a moment. The bitten edge. Can
we zoom in on the bacteria? Don't worry. It's not

going to be significant. It's just a way of holding the fort.

Matthew, putting the key in the lock, a little bit pleased with himself to have bought not only laundry stuff but also a fillet of Kobe beef for no particular reason except Thursday, knows straight away, the second he opens the door. He knows by the song that's playing in the bedroom. He knows by something about the light. He knows that he knows before he even really knows.

He doesn't freak out. He closes the door, he goes into the kitchen, he puts the shopping down on the work surface, he knows, he knows, he knows.

Can't he just call out 'I'm home babe', 'Baby I'm home', what does he usually say?, if he could just say that, and get an answer come back. 'I'm in here babes.' 'Babes come and look at this.'

Oh. I can't write this part.

[Silence.]

I'm sitting at my desk in front of the window that looks out over the street where I live in London and a kid, a Hasidic kid, walks past on the pavement on the far side of the street, and then no one, no one, and I don't want to write this part, and I can't.

I was worried that this would happen. Trying to write this thing.

It's just hard. Go for a walk around the block. Clear my head.

*   *   *

Rehan's never been so relieved to lock the door and turn the sign around to say 'Sorry we're CLOSED!'. He can't wait to waste the evening on a six-pack of Export and *Assassin's Creed IV*. Maybe he'll call his brother in Rawalpindi and take the piss out of him for a bit.

He's shutting everything down for the night and he goes over to turn off the photocopier, but instead of turning it off, he presses the GO button, and the photocopier does a copy of nothing, the paper comes out and lies in the arms of the delivery thing, and he does it again, and again, and he watches the copies of nothing come out and lie in the thing, and he picks one up and looks at it. A picture of the things in the nothing. Lint and hair and dust and miscellaneous sprinkles. And he can feel the warmth coming off the paper and he holds it to his cheek just for a second. Warm and blank.

Graeme is standing at the sink, doing the washing up, looking out of his kitchen window at the road.

The soundtrack tonight is Poulenc. A little bit racy for Classic FM but it is only the slow movement.

That's the fourth time Rufus has been past Graeme's window on his new bike. Of course you only know it's the fourth if you're counting.

Graeme notices his mouth is dry. He'll have a lemon squash when he's finished the dishes. Maybe a little piece of nougat. Nou-gat. Pou-lenc.

Brian, alone in his apartment, listening to the same Poulenc, feels his phone vibrate in his pocket and thinks about ignoring it but can't. The screen display says 'Ben (h)', 'h' for home, and straight away Brian knows. Because if it really was his son calling he'd call from his mobile, he always does, on those rare occasions. So this is Matthew, presumably, from the landline. And so he knows.

They don't talk for long and Brian thanks Matthew very carefully, like he's minding his manners, and then Matthew's gone and Brian watches himself from a great height, an interplanetary distance, watches himself not know whether to sit down or stand up. He does both. Neither.

The Poulenc is so corny. But the room would be silent otherwise.

Rufus finally pulls up right outside Graeme's window. He takes out his phone, looks at it. Holds it out, framing a selfie. Looks right at Graeme. Right at him. Graeme doesn't move. He can't tell but he doesn't think Rufus can really see him through the gaps in the Venetian blind.

Rufus smiles at Graeme, then at the phone. He starts to pull up his T-shirt. Graeme shuts the blind in a hurry. The music plays.

It occurs to Brian he should have said, I'll be right over. I'll be right there. Don't worry, he should have said. He just said thank you.

Second-rate little Tadzio, thinks Graeme, with a tight little smile. Dirty little Poundshop Tadzio.

Matthew crying so fucking hard. Literally banging his head against the wall as he cries. It hardly makes a sound.

The block I'm walking around happens to take me past the Birdcage, where I've said I can't go for a drink tonight with the boys because I'm writing this, which I can't. So they're all there and they're happy to see me when I walk in.

– Christophe!, says Paul.

– Big guy!, says Tassos.

– Chrissy Goo!, says Eddy.

I say, Hey! How's everyone doing?

– Oh fucking hell, says Tim.

What? I say.

– Your fucking catchphrase, says Tim.

What?

– 'Hey! How's everyone doing?'

Is that not all right?, I say.

– It's such bullshit, says Tim. He's obviously quite a lot drunker than everyone else.

Hang on, I say, and I get myself a vodka tonic, and I sit with them, and I say: All right, mouth. What's bullshit?

– It's such fucking bullshit, says Tim. 'How's everyone doing?' is what you say when you don't want to know the answer. Because if anyone ever answered. Like really. Cos we're all so fucked. He's fucked.

He's pointing at Eddy.

– I'm not fucked, says Eddy.

– We're all fucked, says Tim. What if I actually told you how I'm doing and you actually listened and you felt like it was somehow something to actually do with you.

– You're fucked, says Eddy to Tim. You're completely fucked.

We all laugh. Even Tim laughs, eventually. His teeth are definitely fucked.

Matthew calls back asking for a number for Sandra. Brian hasn't got one. She's in Seattle still, as far as he knows. Henry will know, says Brian. And then he tells Matthew he's coming over.

The police are there. Matthew is sort of vibrating. He keeps bursting into tears of course. It's surprising every time. He looks so incredibly alive that Brian thinks, I wish it had been you, you fucking ponce, you gayboy.

Brian doesn't really ask about the sequence of events, and Matthew doesn't say. They agree that Ben seemed happy the last time they saw him. But they both know that's not true. They just don't know how they know.

The young WPC's radio keeps erupting with chatter that no one can understand. Except her, maybe. There are times, thinks Brian, watching Matthew sobbing uncontrollably, there are nights when every conversation sounds like that. Like drivel on a walkie-talkie.

Jeff feels sick, deep down. The theatrical red of those blooded hands. He turns *Newsnight* off. He happens to have picked up the remote with his left hand and he sees the small pink blotch on the back of his hand.

Too late now, he thinks. I'll do it tomorrow.

I've gone back to Eddy's. I have no idea why. I sort of know why. I sort of know what's coming. Eddy's straight but he's more drunk than straight and more lonely than anyone I know. He's sort of *on* loneliness like some people are *on* dialysis.

Full disclosure: I'm not undrunk myself. He's telling me, what the fuck he telling me, he's telling me that Coldplay and Snow Patrol are like the Beethoven of... whatever. He's like, all those people holding their phones up, that's phenomenal. And I'm a snob for wanting them all to fucking... not.

We get back to his. He puts the overhead light on. He has no lamps. I'd forgotten this. He has no lamps in his flat. Just the overhead. He's saying have I ever heard Snow Patrol doing the live version of 'Run' from the Union Chapel. I'm like, no, Eddy, it's really not my thing.

He goes over to his iPod dock and puts it on. He's going to convert me, he says.

I'm standing in the middle of Eddy's living room looking at a picture on the wall, of New York, a black and white photo of New York. It's the kind of photo that comes free with the frame.

The song starts playing and I'm looking at New York where I've never been and I'm thinking about Philip Seymour Hoffman.

Eddy's standing behind me and in my head it's 9.40am and Philip Seymour Hoffman is going into the Standard Grill at the Standard Hotel to have brunch with three men, including two teenagers. Eddy touches the back of my head and now I'm thinking of Woody Allen.

In my head Woody Allen is smiling at his daughter, who is seven years old, and it's 10.57am and Philip Seymour Hoffman is settling the bill for approximately $123, and it's 11.03 and he's leaving the hotel. Eddy's breath on my neck and then his teeth, biting, kissing, his hand on my shoulder, turning me round to face him.

And in my head Woody Allen is taking his daughter by the hand and leading her upstairs into a dim attic on the second floor of the house, and it's about 11.45am and Philip Seymour Hoffman is buying groceries at D'Agostino's on Greenwich Avenue close

to his home and the groceries come to approximately
$142 and Eddy's mouth tastes like booze and sour
milk and his face is scratchy and I'm thinking about
Flight MH370.

And in my head Woody Allen is telling his daughter
to lie on her stomach and play with her brother's
train set, and it's around 8pm and Philip Seymour
Hoffman is back outside D'Agostino's talking to two
people with shoulder bags and it's 12.32 and the pilot
is saying: Ground, MAS370. You are unreadable. Say
again.

Eddy's unbuttoning my red checked shirt and putting
his hand on my chest and in my head Woody Allen
is promising his daughter that they'll go to Paris
and she'll star in his movies and the train is running
in circles around the attic, and Philip Seymour
Hoffman's estranged partner speaks to him on the
phone and he appears to be under the influence of
drugs, and it's 12.40 and the pilot is saying: 32 Right
Cleared for take-off MAS370. Thank you bye.

In my mind Woody Allen is putting his head in his
daughter's naked lap and breathing in and breathing
out, and Eddy's stooped over a bit, sucking my nipple,
and his teeth are jagged and making me flinch, and
Philip Seymour Hoffman is standing at the ATM,
making one more cash withdrawal, totalling $1,200
which will never be found, and it's 1.07 and the pilot
is saying: Malaysian Three Seven Zero maintaining
level three five zero and Eddy's undoing my belt and
unbuttoning my jeans and pushing his hand down
the back of my pants.

And it's 11.36 and screenwriter David Bar Katz and
assistant Isabella Wing-Davey find Philip Seymour
Hoffman in his bathroom, unconscious and lying on
his right side, and Eddy's forcing a finger into me,

dry, like raw, and there's a big round of applause for Snow Patrol, and it's 1.19 and the pilot says: Good night Malaysian Three Seven Zero, and in my mind Woody Allen is breathing in and out and breathing in and out and breathing.

*   *   *

Four nights and two showers and a Sunday night bath and the small pink blotch on Jeff's hand is still there, that must have been permanent marker as in really forever.

And again he's awake long before the radio wakes him. Maybe this is forever now too, for always, every dawn. Vigilantly waiting for the deleted milkman.

When Rehan does the papers, the headline on the first bundle is: DADDY, MY HERO.

That word ricochets around Rehan's head. DADDY. DADDY. He has to say it aloud – DADDY – to stop it. Like breaking a spell.

David Cameron has gone on holiday.

Jeff already knows he's going to be very late for work. He calls the woman.

7.03. Rehan opens up. Derrick is waiting.

– You're five minutes late, bruv, says Derrick.

– I think you're running a little fast there, my friend, says Rehan.

– It's on purpose, says Derrick. That's how I maintain my competitive advantage. Have you got mouthwash?

– No, says Rehan. Chemists for that.

– You've got johnnies, says Derrick.

– You know me, says Rehan. Always the romantic.

The front page of Derrick's newspaper is split down the middle. On the left is a picture of the soldier's widow crying and it says HELL. On the right is David Cameron and his wife having breakfast in Ibiza and it says HOL. So it says HELL | HOL.

– You should get mouthwash, says Derrick. You'd make a killing.

Arthur is sitting on the wall round by the netball court. He's re-watching Saturday night's UFC on his phone. Velasquez v Bigfoot. Everybody else is in registration. And then up walks Rufus, who's late, and Rufus says: What are you watching? And he climbs up on the wall and sits next to Arthur and they're both looking at this little screen and the stupid buffering.

They're sitting so close to each other on the wall that Rufus can hear sounds going on inside Arthur's body.

The next voice is the Deputy Head.

– Carry on at break, says Arthur.

– Fucking excellent, says Rufus.

Jeff, still in his pyjamas, climbs up into the attic. When was the last time he was up here? Everything about it feels strange. Not unfamiliar, just strange.

And there of course is all of Annie's stuff. The idea was it would go to the Sue Ryder but anyway.

He looks for a while in the wrong place, though he knows where the right place is. Then he looks in the right place.

Unmarked white cardboard box, like a little coffin. And in it is Prissy. Annie's black doll, named by her uncle after the maid from *Gone With The Wind*. Butterfly McQueen with her little girl's voice. Prissy tucked up in her box in her white frock, her frills and buttons. Ugly little perisher, but precious.

– Prissy, says Jeff, very quietly, like he doesn't want to wake her.

Graeme closes his eyes for a moment after lunch and micro-dreams that the air has cancer. You can see it. It looks like ripples.

The cut above Arthur's eye is admittedly bleeding a lot, sort of glamorously. Rufus isn't really sure how it happened. There was just the roar of his absolute unconditional love for Arthur. And then there was blood on the wall of the cubicle, and all on the floor, and on Rufus's sleeve. And Arthur crying without making any sound, sitting on the toilet floor with his pants still down around his knees. Blood on his shirt.

You just fell, Rufus is telepathically insisting across the playground as Arthur tells miss. You just fell. Maybe I fell onto you, yes.

But Arthur's pointing at Rufus and miss is looking over.

Rufus puts his hand in his back pocket. Forty quid of birthday money still right there.

He's over the railings before miss has even got her shit together.

Jeff and Prissy avoiding the main roads. Prissy in her box on the passenger seat. There's a funny metallic taste in Jeff's mouth. He's joining in with the pop quiz on Radio 2.

A few spots of rain on the windscreen.

– Simply Red, says Jeff.

Grim-looking birds on the power lines.

– Marty Wilde, says Jeff. No, Billy Fury.

Diabetic travel sweets on the shelf above the glove compartment.

– Tip of my tongue, says Jeff.

Five, four, three, says the radio. Two. One.

– Tears for Fears, says Jeff, in the nick of time.

Rufus gets a boner on the train, thinking about the blood on Arthur's shirt and what he looked like on the ground. And because he's going to London where everyone has sex like constantly.

For your own comfort and safety, says a notice, please keep your feet off the seats.

Rufus puts his hand down his trousers and thinks about what tattoo he wants when he's older.

Someone's been practising their tag on the window in bright pink sharpie. MUT-8. MUT-8. With an 8. And someone else has tried to scratch it out and they can't so they've just scratched CUNT. No curves. All angles.

– Cunt, says Rufus out loud to the carriage, cordially, like it's Hello or Many happy returns.

The car park area at the edge of the woods feels very sad to Jeff, even on a sunny day like this.

He doesn't know whether to carry Prissy in her box or not. It's going to look weird either way. Man with a little white cardboard coffin walking into the woods. Or a man holding a black doll by the hand. Or by the neck.

He gets a Morrisons bag out of the boot, puts Prissy in the bag. Checks for air holes.

Rufus hasn't thought about what he's going to actually do.

The train has arrived at Liverpool Street. He gets a 7-Up at Whistlestop and decides he'll just follow the first good-looking man he sees.

It doesn't take long. It turns out to be a labourer of some kind, in high-vis and steel cap boots. And other clothes. This isn't porn, not everything's porn.

He follows the labourer down on to the Underground, close enough behind him to sneak through the ticket barriers, which means close enough to smell this guy, his body, his work smell. The smell makes Rufus want to just follow this guy for ever, down into the depths.

But there's a big poster on the platform, big red letters that Rufus eventually figures out say NONALIGNMENT PACT and then in smaller letters underneath it says: Punk / Post-Punk / Politics 1976-1983. And there's a picture of a nude woman with an iron where her head should be, and grinning lipsticked mouths pasted over her tits. And the name of a gallery and the closest tube.

I'm going there, thinks Rufus, and he dumps the labourer like a leaky binbag.

– That's where we did it, says Jeff, pointing at a tree on the other side of the clearing. He and Prissy are sitting side by side under another tree, taking it all in.

– She kept saying we mustn't, we shouldn't, says Jeff, we shouldn't, I can't remember, we mustn't, something like that. She didn't say no. I'd have stopped if she'd said no. But she just said we shouldn't, or we mustn't. You know, in case someone came along. I had, I must admit, I had thought of it as romantic. To… ravish her, like that, in the open air, in the woods. The smell of the woods. You don't hear people say 'ravish' any more, do you?

It's very quiet in the woods. A hissing sound at the bottom of the silence. Like something seething.

– No you don't, says Prissy, in a man's voice. It's not something that gets said any more.

– She never said no and she never said stop, says Jeff. I thought she'd get caught up in the moment.

– When was this again?, says Prissy

– Um, May, June, 1971, says Jeff. There'd been an earthquake in Turkey or somewhere. She was a bit upset. I don't know why. The Sunday, we said let's go out for a drive. We came here.

I regret it in a way, says Jeff. I don't think she really wanted to. But then I think if she'd actually, you know, whatever the word… consented, I think I would have… I wouldn't have seen it through. It would have taken the sting out of it. Does that make sense?

– Yeah, says Prissy. Yeah it does make sense.

'Contains work of an adult nature', says the notice by the ticket desk. 'Children under 16 must be accompanied.'

Full price £11.50, it says.

Literally everything on the notice can fuck itself. Rufus walks past the desk, past the woman, past the guard. He's got a line ready if anyone should challenge him, but nobody does.

Inside it's like an arcade or something. Competing sounds and lights and a sense of swirling movement. This is not like the gallery Rufus went to before, with school. He can feel something here already.

On a video screen in the first space, a naked man covered in blood or ketchup is moaning in a dim, confusing room. It sounds like he might be throwing up. The man looks a bit like Rufus's maths teacher.

In the same space, a big photo of another naked man, cropped off at the pubic hair, but he's much hotter, this guy, Rufus has no teachers that look like this. If he did he'd go to school more often.

And there's a black-and-white photo of a man in a leather mask pissing into a bearded man's mouth, which is like OK, and right next to that there's a sort of cartoon of a red man with yellow hair and a yellow man with red hair and the red man's red cock is sticking in the yellow man's mouth and the yellow man's yellow cock is sticking in the red man's mouth and their balls are fuzzy and in the corner it says HUNGER and it's so rude that Rufus can't stop giggling. Which makes some of the other adults who are looking at it giggle too but Rufus is also thinking, if I drew that, I'd get a week of detention.

And there's a photograph of a naked man sitting smoking a cigarette on someone's bed and the light on him is also red and yellow and it's very pretty and Rufus sees that the guy who took the photograph is called Nan Goldin and he thinks what a funny name for a man.

And there's an old black-and-white photo of some kind of scuffle between these smartly dressed men and then on top of that it says: 'You construct intricate rituals which allow you to touch the skin of other men.' Rufus looks at that one for a while and he thinks about what it says and in the end he thinks: not *that* intricate.

They've lapsed into silence, Jeff and Prissy. Jeff's heart's going bang bang bang. It's surprising. This must be what it's like to tell your mother you're a puff.

– I hope…, says Prissy. I hope you know you can tell me anything.

Jeff looks down at her. Her unblinking little glass eyes. Her unopening little mouth.

– I know, he says. We go back a long way.

– I know you're a good man, says Prissy. Jeff is a bit choked.

– Thank you, he says. You were very precious to Annie.

You won't have seen, says Jeff, but there's been a bit of bother with a soldier. These two Muslim lads. British. Emphasis on the 'ish'. Both called Michael. Michael Adebo-something and Michael Adebo-something-else. Just set about this soldier with a…

His mind can't retrieve the word for a moment.

– Like a hatchet but you'd do livestock with it. … Cleaver. A cleaver. Tried to get his head off. Run him over with a car first. Fucking Vauxhall Tigra! Pardon my language.

So the guy's dead and this small crowd gathers around the body and one of them phones Michael Ade-doodah, not phones him, films him on their phone, videos him, and he… speaks. His hands…

I dreamt about his hands one night. Dreamt his hands had jewels on. Covered in jewels.

He speaks, this bastard. I think I can call him a bastard in the context.

He says… You know, we done this because, you know, British soldiers kill Muslims every day. He's like, you started this war. You wanted this war. So this is what this is. He says you're, you know, you call us extremists. You're the extremists. We're just fighting the war you started.

He says it all a lot more eloquently than I'm saying it.

And he's standing there. Blood on his hands. Not trying to get away, run away. Standing there, like, standing… Like when you stand. Your ground.

I'm not being funny but.

I'm 73 years old. I did my National Service, I was one of the last. Came out, worked as best I could. I was a bit lost. Met my Annie. You know. You know what that meant.

Did my best. Did all right. Not spectacular. We weren't blessed with children, as you know. So that's a shame. That's a fucking shame. Because it means you have to find a different story to tell about your life.

Annie. She was… That was the story I told. And you get lied to. And the wind changes. She never changed. Till the end. That was a quick change.

And I look around. When I remember to look up. I look around. And I don't expect it to be the same.

See these boys out on the street marching for whatever the hell they think they're marching for. Against the Muslims. Against, I don't know, whatever they're against. Against themselves, I sometimes think.

Me and them, we were told the same lies by the same scumbags but we came to different conclusions.

And now I just I'm here talking to you because I'm so incredibly alone and I'm lost, I'm lost. Prissy I've lost the thread of my story. Cos Annie went and now I'm on my own and I'm looking at these Muslim lads, I'm reading this speech in the paper, I'm hearing it on the news, day after day on the news, these bits of this speech about we're the extremists and they're just

fighting the war we started and I look at it all and I
think, well, yeah.

I think, yeah. I agree. I can't disagree.

I think those boys out marching don't speak for me.

That bastard with the blood on his hands. He speaks
for me.

I'd stand with him.

Don't get me wrong, I hope they throw away the key,
but I think he's fucking right, and I sort of think what
they did was… valiant, and I'm 73 and my wife's
gone and who the fuck do I tell. About that then.

Prissy.

He looks down at Prissy and Prissy is his wife's old
black doll, sitting under a tree.

And Jeff for a moment lets his guard down and
out comes a sound like a wolf. He makes a sound
just like a fucking wolf. Like he's never heard. He's
been harbouring that sound, all this time, like you'd
harbour a criminal.

Large and isolated on a grey wall, three panels, on
each of which is a figure. A slightly less than lifesize
man in a sharp black suit, white shirt, black tie, black
shoes. And each man is drawn contorted in a different
way, in his own way, flailing. As though falling, or
fallen, or twisted somehow or bent.

Rufus looks at the first contorted man. And at the second. And the third. And the first and the second. And the second and the third. And the first and the second and the third. Each of these men. Looking at them in the way that he only ever looks at the very most fucked-up desperate porn. Intimately like an aiport scanner. Wanting to mingle with the information.

His eyes are wet. Fuck that.

He goes up to the small white card next to the left-hand panel.

It says: Robert Longo, b.1953. MEN IN THE CITIES. 1980. Charcoal and graphite on paper.

He steps back. Looks again from a few feet away, at the three contorted men.

The rush in his head. The roar.

The capacity for love. The need for injury.

Every sofa on fire for ever in every car park at the edge of every woods.

And it's Monday 27th May 2013, which is my fortieth birthday. I've told everyone I'm going to be out of town, but I lied.

There's no one in the world that knows where I am.

2.

Jeff doesn't even bother turning the radio off when it comes on. He just turns over in bed and goes back to sleep and it carries on telling the news to no one.

Derrick's waited outside the shop until quarter past seven. But Rehan doesn't open up. Derrick goes to Costcutter. He misses the banter but the milk's 4p cheaper.

It's the Friday before Christmas. Graeme stands at his kitchen window waiting for the kettle to boil. All down the street in other windows there are lights flashing on and off, chasing each other round. It's all so vulgar, thinks Graeme. Christmas is just sugary piss these days. He's done a little tree but it's very understated. One really wants to be able to think about Christ, once in a while. The star and the magi.

Tom is trying to bite the top off a plastic bottle of milk because the little tag's come off. Che is looking around his mum's place for stuff he can take to Cash Converters. Albert misses Talbot.

On the screen of Rufus's phone, a bony emo boy is getting a prodigious faceful of cum off a lad called Aaron who's the newest superstar on Gay Twink Angels. He's making out it's like the nicest cum he's ever tasted, like it's really really nice. Rufus isn't watching. He's in the bathroom, crying his eyes out.

In a flat across town, the same cumshot is playing out on a larger screen, a desktop computer on an immaculately tidy desk. Brian comes in and switches off the monitor, shuts down the computer. Switches it off at the wall. Time he wasn't here. He's got to go up to London for a meeting.

Michael Adebolajo and Michael Adebowale are guilty of the murder of Drummer Lee Rigby of the Royal Regiment of Fusiliers. Lord Justice Sweeney says he can't pass sentence until January, when an appeal court decision is due on the use of whole-life tariffs.

I'm writing this sitting at my desk which is covered in books and papers and sweetie wrappers and CDs without sleeves and I'm watching a video of David Cameron talking about whole-life sentences. He says:

What I believe is very clear. There are some people who commit such dreadful crimes that they should be sent to prison and life should mean life.

– Come on Roof, shouts Rufus's stepdad up the stairs. Time we weren't here.

– You're quiet, says Rufus's stepdad once they're in the car. Let's give him a name now. Nigel. Neil.

No one likes the dentist, says Neil.

Neither of them notices that Rufus's small fists are clenched on his knees.

– When we get back, says Neil, why don't you take your bike out for a spin? I haven't seen you out on it in ages.

– It's a bit pointless, says Rufus.

When they get to the dental surgery, Rufus sits in the waiting room while Neil goes to the bathroom.

He doesn't need a piss, he needs a moment.

He washes his hands, splashes water on his face. Looks at himself looking back.

You try to make things work. You never know what you're taking on.

He dries his hands in the hand drier, which is another way of not going out there again for another few seconds.

And then he goes back out and along the corridor and there's Rufus, sitting on a too-small chair at a table in the corner of the waiting room. There's this toy thing on the table, all these intertwining lines and you move blocks around the lines. There's no skill involved. Just an incredibly limited set of options for playing. To keep the littl'uns amused and distracted. It would bore a child of six. And there's Rufus, moving these blocks around. Totally unselfconscious. Concentrating hard. His face looks calm and handsome.

Where's he gone?, thinks Neil. Where's he gone to?

– I'm so sorry I'm late, says Brian. He's not late. But saying 'hello' will sound too chipper.

– You're not late, says Matthew. I was early.

– You picked a good bench, says Brian.

– I really like the view from up here, says Matthew.

Brian sits down next to him and they look out over London together. All these different buildings, different styles, like a brawl. St Pancras, and St Paul's looking tiny these days and the fucking Shard, the fucking Shard, that should actually be its official name, the Fucking Shard, that's all it does all day, fuck the sky with its jagged edge. Brian looks at the sky. Fuck the sky. Weird stupid clods of matter moving around arbitrarily in the fucked sky which he knows are birds but honestly they just look like stupid unnecessary dirt or something, or unused letters in a foreign alphabet.

– Thanks for meeting me, says Brian. How are you doing?

– I'm OK, says Matthew. Settling in. Good to be here. In the city, I mean.

– What's the new job?, asks Brian. But he doesn't listen as Matthew witters on about it all. He waits for it to stop so he can ask his question.

– I wanted to ask you something, says Brian. I hope you won't be offended. I just don't know who to ask.

– Please, says Matthew.

– I've been looking at a couple of web sites, says Brian, in the past few weeks. Well one in particular.

I don't know if you know it. I'm afraid it's called Gay Twink Angels.

Matthew laughs. – I've heard of it, he says.

– I've been… Rather a lot, and I joined, with my credit card, and I just wanted to check, that sort of thing, it's not illegal is it? I mean they say it's not illegal if you're over eighteen but it seems such a grey area from what I can understand, especially when it's younger people, and I just, I, I, I don't want to get my door kicked in at six in the morning. Or any time of the morning.

– No one will kick your door down, Brian, says Matthew. No one cares.

– Oh thank God, says Brian. I know it's stupid. I'm not, it's not a gay thing, it's not sexual, I just… I hope it's not wrong to say this, says Brian. But… You and Ben.

Two little girls go past on pink scooters, not at any speed but laughing gaily.

– I always had a sense that you were happy together, says Brian. And I'm not very good at happy. Or together. And I happened to get an email, a spam thing, and it led me down a bit of a path and there was… I saw a scene from Gay Twink Angels and the boys were so happy. Or seemed happy. I couldn't believe it was faked. They seemed genuinely happy. These American… sissies, I suppose I'd call them. Laughing and happy. Unashamed. You think of all the other people who are there, you know, the director, the cameraman, the sound man. All these men. And in the middle of it all, just what seems to be actual happiness. They're all arms and legs. Well not all. But I'm finding it very… What's the word? Consoling.

Mending. I feel mended by it. Held. I feel very stupid telling you.

Brian looks down the hill. There's a big tree and underneath a bunch of fat women are doing t'ai chi. They look ridiculous.

I'm in my room. I've got some music on. I still can't write this thing.

I call my dad.

– Only me, I say.

– Hello me, he says, which is kind of a running joke but it also covers the few seconds it takes him to remember my name.

– I was a bit wary, he says. I get a lot of cold calls.

– Yes I know, I say. How are you keeping?

– Bit coldy, he says.

– That's rotten, I say. Listen I was wondering if I could come home for a few days.

– Of course, he says.

– I'm trying to write this thing, I say. I'm a bit stuck.

– I'd love to have you, he says.

– I thought a change of scene would do me good.

– You'd be most welcome, he says.

– I don't want to put you out, I say, and it's only as I'm remembering this conversation that I realise by this point he's already said three times that it's fine.

– It's fine, he says. Really. When would you like to come?

– Sort of now, I say. Is that all right?

Matthew is watching the birds. How stunning they are, just ordinary birds. He's looking at the Shard. What amazing energy. Look at it. What a skyline. This city.

He tunes back in to Brian.

– But there aren't, are there, says Brian.

– Aren't what?

– Aren't reasons, he says. That's the hardest thing to accept. There's no whys or wherefores. Other people, the people you care about, they're, you know, they can be ever so close and you still don't know. You'll never know. It took me weeks to understand.

– Understand what?, says Matthew. I'm sorry, I don't follow.

– To understand that Ben made his decision and that was his decision and it… It wasn't… I thought it had to be my fault, somehow. But it wasn't.

Matthew bites his fingernail for a moment. Takes his finger away from his mouth and there's a tiny bead of blood on his finger, like a little red sequin, a tiny little jewel.

– Yeah but it was, he says to Brian, softly. It was your fault.

Everything about him was damaged, says Matthew. You know that. You know that. You know it. Where do you think that came from? It was absolutely your fault.

And he goes. Like that. And he's gone.

My dad picks me up from the station.

– How's the car performing?, I say. It's one of the things we talk about in the car.

My dad's in his eighties now. He's got new dentures. His smile has completely changed. He sort of has a bit of the strangeness of other people's dads about him now.

He's getting a bit forgetful. Or more than. You know. He goes into a familiar room, he can't always find his way out again, just for a second.

I love him. I do love him. I don't know what comes next.

Brian is fucked. Gin and mulled wine and pear cider because he's never tried it and it slips down very easily doesn't it. And his heart is broken but we knew that.

And then he's out in the street, in the main road, Christmas illuminations and London traffic, barrelling his way down the pavement, everyone getting out of his way. There are so many people. So many people. What a lot of people. Doing their shopping and their Christmas drinks and their inexplicable lives.

It doesn't sound like this.

It sounds like this.

[The sound of traffic, and of people.]

And above this staggering chaos he hears a voice cut through, singing –

And he thinks the voice has come from inside him, like a haemorrhage or something, and then he hears it again –

And it's definitely outside him and he looks up and he tries to focus and there in the Christmas lights all of six foot nine and dressed in a white vest and denim cut-offs in the winter cold and black boots and a black studded halo is a bona fide Gay Twink Angel, singing –

Of course, thinks Brian. This is the beginning of something true, at last. And he raises his voice above the crowd to tell the angel everything.

– HEY FRIEND hey pal hey supernatural radiant bender! Take my freedom, please! It's just a joke now, just a lame joke. Hey glowing vest-clad faggot of uncertain origin! Hey sex derangement hallucination child-of-our-time! Mixed-reality space sentinel amid bloodstreaked effigies of Christmas disillumination! Messenger of absolute guiltless self-immolation in the very place of these swirling international crowds! Why won't you hurt me more? Oh sorrow, sorrow, Angel! Create will you somehow not upon this convoluted rattling unmitigable breath. I need to try and speak all the language out of my mouth! – you toxic shining boy, you hanging-over-me threat of disappearance, dissolution, of splitting up like a failed marriage, my atoms are so stuck in this stupid configuration. // *And my father and his father and his father.* // Won't you read me? Won't you drag me by the tongue into whatever oblivion will have me now? I must get this poison out of my life, decommission this terrible apparatus. I have to re-hurt the wound that sprung me. I have to beg for the forgiveness of my son, that happy skeleton. Take my freedom, for God's sake! Can't I be destroyed by you? By some infinitely beautifully unsafe sexually-transmitted vengeance? I have been a banal municipal architect, a disappointment to every creature, a waste of counterfeit pain; I have lied, I have stolen, I have withdrawn into my own sadness, I have spoken in favour of privatisation; I have ridiculed my own son for his desperate beauty. Unmistake my freedom here and now for the egregious desolation that was all it ever signified. I need to cough it all up, somehow, the tar of this lack of love! I need to disembowel myself, hands-free: 1st hurt my own hands, but speak my interior into some blessed flatline. // Shard me, Angel! Shard me into loving blackness, into the long night solstice. *My father and his father and his father.* Shard me out of this dilapidated existence. Why can't it hurt more? Why won't you hurt me even more? Will you come in a thousand animal bodies to trample me in a great stampede? Will you come like a cutthroat robber to steal me away from my humiliated self? Won't you hear my need for unhealing? For unwholeness? Don't be sad, Angel! I am giving myself to joy! To be torn apart by necessary eagles and homophobes! Away with my bottled self, my kevlar and polystyrene soul, my detested uniform self, my hateful musculature, my ignorance and fear (*my father and his father and his father*) back to the primal texts of dread and the connivance of men with men to abolish the starfleet. // CREATE UPON MY FLESH sings Gay Twink Angel to his cowed disgraced disciple in the hard heart of the city, no snowfall, no firmament, only useless antibiotics and the diseases they no longer cure. Sing out, Angel! Let disavowal crash about my head, a cacophony of repudiation: I cannot hold what I am given, I am sad with metal fatigue and the collapsing ceiling of the Apollo Theatre. Take my hopeless mesmerising freedom! Strip it out of me. Deliver me from the fearsome mercy of the universal order that gives us only and exactly that for which we ask, with our ravaged bodies and our pollutants and our children who would rather die than forgive us or let us speak to them directly of the animals we once were, the magnificent wretched animals traipsing over dark forest floors towards firelight and sex and entropy. // TAKE TAKE TAKE TAKE TAKE IT. // Take my sickness and my delight, it's all the same, it's all implicated in the tumbling away, in the turning, in the draining away of the lifeblood. // TAKE TAKE TAKE TAKE TAKE IT. // ~~My father and his father and his father.~~ // And the hoping heart battered into spreadsheet-shapes, the optimistic nervous system stalled at the gate: we cannot survive by 3D printing alone, we cannot survive on Snow Patrol and Operation Yewtree and chewable Methylin: we cannot survive on eye-test charts and *is the red circle clearer than the green circle and is this better with or without and is the green circle clearer than the red circle and how about now is it better with or without?* I am pleading with you, Angel, better without, without!

// O TAKE TAKE TAKE TAKE TAKE IT. // Put us
ardently into reverse. Make the Shard into an abattoir.
Let the ghosts of us fuck what they can. Let the dogs
overrun our culture and shit in our cathedrals. Come
on fuck me up Angel with whatever you have that's
jagged, with your knuckledustered hand, with your
cheapskate Portland Saturday Market accessories,
there is no imaginable shame of which I do not
strive to be worthy, Angel. It cannot possibly hurt
enough. Not even time in its gutless pomp can hurt
me enough. // ~~And my father and his father and his
father.~~ // AND ALL THE PEOPLE WHO ARE
KILLED BY VENDING MACHINES. AND
ALL THE PEOPLE WHO ARE TORTURED
OVERSEAS SO THAT MY SON CAN HAVE
AN EDUCATION TO HURL HIMSELF OUT
OF. AND ALL THE PEOPLE WHO ONLY
WANTED A KISS SO THAT THAT COULD BE
SOMETHING WORTH REMEMBERING. AND
ALL THE PEOPLE PULLING EACH OTHER
UP OUT OF THEIR OWN GRAVES ON THAT
DAY. AND ALL THE PEOPLE TAKING THEIR
CLOTHES OFF IN MY MIND. AND YOU,
ANGEL, IN MY MIND, TAKING OFF YOUR
CLOTHES, AND SMILING, AND APPEARING
<u>HAPPY</u>, AND <u>WITHOUT SORROW</u>, AND
<u>WOULD YOU DO IT FOR FREE</u>?

*   *   *

Jeff in his sitting-room watching the evening news.

Me and my dad, in my dad's sitting-room, watching the same news.

Two old straight white ex-servicemen, a hundred and eighty miles apart, joined at the screen.

Michael Adebolajo's face more familiar to me now in a way than my dead mother or even my father who is right there next to me with a new smile that he's not smiling.

David Cameron on the screen, this clip of him talking about sentencing, about life should mean life.

OK. Jeff gets up and goes into the kitchen.

My dad gets up and goes into his kitchen.

Jeff puts the kettle on. He leans against the sink unit.

My dad starts filling the washing-up bowl.

Jeff exits the kitchen. Off upstairs. We can't see him for a bit. We're not going to follow him.

My dad giving the Fairy liquid a parsimonious squeeze.

Talking heads on the subject of whole-life sentences. Someone saying about the possibility of redemption. That doesn't go over well.

Jeff coming back downstairs in a hurry. He slides open the back door and goes out onto the patio. The rush of cold air into the warm room.

Jeff is holding Prissy by the throat. He puts her down on the patio. He stamps on her face. Twice. Three times. Four times. Her face is destroyed. He stamps on her belly. Her belly is destroyed.

He shouts in her destroyed face.

He comes back into the room. Goes over to the sideboard, to the top drawer, then to the next drawer down. Takes out a black permanent marker. Goes back out onto the patio. He tears Prissy's little white dress away from her broken body.

He shouts in her face again.

On the wreckage of her body and then her head in permanent marker Jeff writes PROSTITUTE. Actually he writes PROSTITE.

He stares into her crumpled face, not knowing whether to spit.

– I always knew you had that in you, says Prissy.

My dad in his kitchen. Something goes smash.

– You all right?, I say.

– Just a plate, he says.

I go out into the kitchen. He's looking befuddled. There are bits of broken plate all over and he's not wearing shoes.

– Don't move, I say. I've got it.

And I crouch down and start to collect up the pieces.

– It's all right, he says. It's my mess, I'll do it.

– You haven't got shoes on, I say. You stay put. I'll be done in a jiffy.

– You haven't got shoes on either, he says. It's my kitchen. It's my mess.

– It's just quicker, isn't it, I say.

– I'll do it! For heaven's sake, says my dad.

– You don't have to, I say. I'm here. Let me help. It's hard enough.

He says: What do you mean, hard enough?

– I mean it's hard enough. Will you not just let me help. Jesus.

And I know my mouth's about to run away with me and I could stop but I don't.

– This fucking bullshit, I say, and he looks like I've slapped him. It's such fucking what do you think is the point, I say. I'm here. I love you. You're old now. You don't know anything about me. There's china everywhere. Look it's gone under the fridge. Just let me help. Just stop being angry and defensive. Every time I come home. It's Christmas. Every time I come home. This war. You don't know what it means when I can't write what I'm trying to write because you don't know anything about me. You don't know how I live. There's nothing anywhere. Just rooms and junk and it's empty. It's all empty. Of anything.

He's crying now, and he looks so strange, and I say:

– Aren't you just fucking tired, Dad. Aren't you just tired. Can't we just put it all down.

I feel my shoulders drop. And I'm pleading with my dad:

– Aren't you just tired, old love. Can't we just put it down. Put it all down and really stop and let it all just be over.

And as I'm saying this he's fading in my imagination, I can't even see him any more. It's just you. All I can see is you there sitting in the dark looking at me and I'm saying:

I know. I know. Can we not just put it all down. Aren't you tired of it all. Aren't you just tired.

Graeme is sight-reading 'Away in a Manger'. Only he hasn't noticed that's supposed to be a B flat all the way through so it sounds a bit wrong.

He wishes it were bed time but it's not quite yet. Maybe he'll read for a while.

Then the sound of something coming through the door. Through the letterbox. This time of night.

He pads out into the hall, and there's a piece of paper on the doormat. He opens the door, takes a step out, looks both ways. Just disappearing out of sight, a red-headed boy riding his bicycle with no hands and no coat on.

Graeme closes the door. He bends to pick up the paper. It's school file paper folded twice into a sort of Christmas card. On the front, a quick crude drawing of a cock and balls. Drops of presumably spunk coming out of the cock. Graeme feels his heart beat in his neck. It's like a physical assault. Which is to say, not unwelcome.

His hands are really shaking as he opens the makeshift Christmas card. He reads the message and his breath goes out of him.

Thank God, he thinks. O God. O thank God. He's never felt so grateful to anyone.

The words in the card, in black felt tip:

INSIDE YOU THERE IS A TERRORIST.

Rod Palladino can't even sleep. He's sick of staring at these walls, this apartment, this smallness, this punishment block. He's going to go out. Take the Subaru for a spin. For a burn. Make something happen. For once, make something actually happen.

He gets dressed, grabs his coat and his keys and heads down to the car park at the back of the apartments. With the overflowing recycling bins and the over-sensitive security lights. And there she is. His gorgeous girl. Well. What's a Christmas bonus for?

One in the morning. No one around. Everyone home in the bosom of their families. Poor fuckers. It crosses his mind as he pictures a family all sitting round the telly that he might be over the limit. By some considerable margin. But it's not going to matter. There's no one out there, is there? Just open roads.

What Rod Palladino hasn't taken into account is that I quite want to kill him. And of course I can. At any moment. A heart attack or a stroke at the wheel or zombies, if I want. I'm so insanely capricious, darling. Mad on authorial power and queer resentment.

Rod Palladino doesn't indicate, doesn't Give Way,
there's nothing to Give Way to. Out onto the dual
carriageway, heading north to nowhere in particular.
197 bhp, two litre engine mounted incredibly low in
the chassis, so you've got this low centre of gravity. It's
truly a delightful drive.

Thinking this calls for some quality tuneage, he turns
on the radio to see what's what. Incredibly wrongly it's
the news and before he can switch to another station
he hears David Cameron, that pudding-faced jamrag,
delivering his catnip soundbite: LIFE SHOULD
MEAN LIFE.

So many stores, thinks Rod Palladino as he drives out
of town, so many stores with their lights on and no
one shopping. These glowing boxes all over the country
like so many crash-landed UFOs. I suppose they get
deliveries at night. You forget about all the people
doing night-shifts. All of them failed in the game of
life, thinks Rod, he thinks this is the life, and he starts
to put his foot down, all that's missing is a beer and
a blowjob, he cracks the window a little bit, feels the
winter air rush in, and it's fucking great, and on comes
Foreigner, 'I Want To Know What Love Is'. Tune!

So listen. What does it mean to create a character only
to kill them off? Isn't that fucking cheap and nasty? Isn't
that every exhausted ironic gesture I ever hated, rolled
into one? The interesting thing is to let him win, Rod
Palladino as he nudges ninety, tearing up the A1017.

Spare his life. Put his kid on the back seat. You won't
kill an innocent child. Here's Freddie with a toy, with a
Big Hugs Elmo, you're not going to hurt Elmo are you.
Daddy, says Freddie. Where are we going? Why are we
going so fast? I'm supposed to be in bed ages ago.

Rod turns up the radio. Daddy slow down, says Freddie. I don't know what you're doing with that fucking Elmo, says Rod to his boy. I told your mum you're too old for that nonsense. I offered to get you a Teksta Dog. Remember? He's going to get so bullied, thinks Rod. Well it might be exactly what's required.

Viewed through the frame of this particular windscreen the road ahead smacks of manifest destiny. Of eating up the miles. Of victory and transcendence and ultimately sleeping the sleep of the just. The erotic spur of forward motion. The rhythms of the road and the lights and LIFE SHOULD MEAN LIFE (David Cameron).

Going for the ton now, Rod Palladino, wanting to give his son and heir something to remember. And then strangely his mind is crowded with clashing memories of childhood. Of red ants and orangeade and Vaseline and playing fort at the dump. What the fuck's this, thinks Rod? Fucking flashback?

– Please Daddy, says Freddie. But Rod's recalling the look in his older brother's eyes, ejaculating onto a stolen copy of *Mayfair* as they jerked off together at the dump. That look. What is that look, that hatred? That hatred in nature? The blaze in those eyes?

– Daddy! Freddie sees the vixen run out into the road. Daddy!

– Fuck, says Rod, and he swerves, and everything goes into action movie slowmo. This is the life, says Rod to no one, as the car spins out of control and then turns over, his son's face splintering into thirty thousand tiny pieces: and only I can save them now.

[Beat.]

Fuck 'em.